Copyright © 2012 Shawn Todd/Blessed Nursery under # 1-8553744511

All rights reserved. No part of this publication may be reproduced, distributed, or transmitted in any form or by any means, including photocopying, recording, or other electronic or mechanical methods, without the prior written permission of the publisher/author, except in the case of breif quotations embodied in critical reviews and certain other noncommercial uses permitted by copyright law. For permission requests, write to the publisher/author, addressed "Attention: Permission Coordinator," at the address or email below.

Blessed Nursery
4210 NE 60th Ct.
Kansas City, MO 64119

Myjesusbook.com

Printed in the United States of America

Second edition 2014,

ISBN- 978-0-615-94076-2

13 Lessons for

Pages 1 and 2 : God the Creator

Pages 3 and 4 : God the Father

Pages 5 and 6 : Jesus loves you

Pages 7 and 8 : Love Jesus

Pages 9 and 10 : Prayer

Pages 11 and 12 : Be kind to others

Pages 13 and 14 : Anything is possible with Jesus

Pages 15 and 16 : Have no fear

God's children

Pages 17 and 18 : Jesus will never leave you

Pages 19 and 20 : Jesus loves everyone

Pages 21 and 22 : Forgive others

Pages 23 and 24 : Jesus thinks you are perfect

Pages 25 and 26 : Obey your parents

Pages 27 and 28 : Always remember

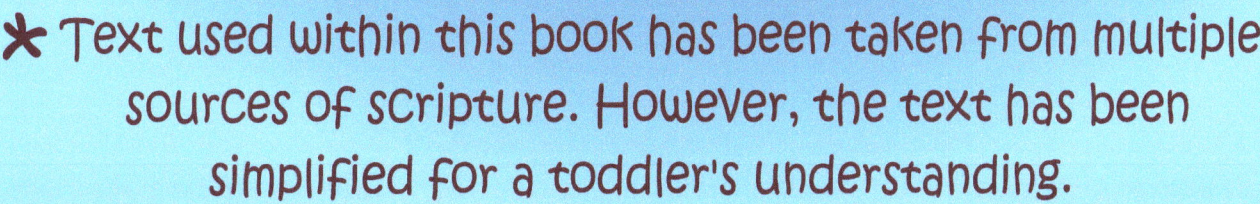

* Text used within this book has been taken from multiple sources of scripture. However, the text has been simplified for a toddler's understanding.

1

God made everything from the Earth to the Sun to the stars and the moon. God even made you.

(Taken from Genesis 1)

God is Jesus' dad.
(Taken from John 10:30)

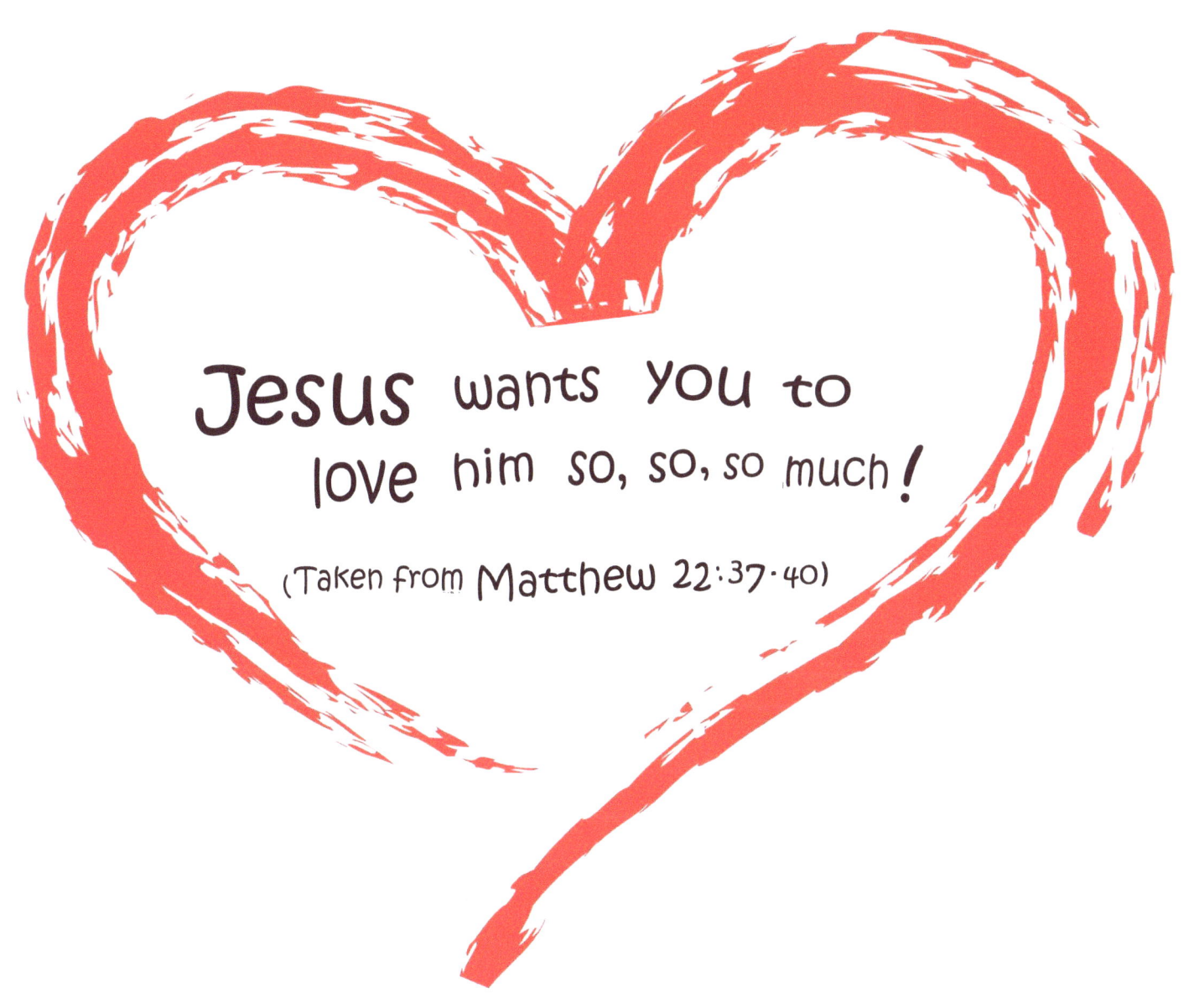

When you pray, Jesus hears every word you say.

(Taken from Psalm 116:1)

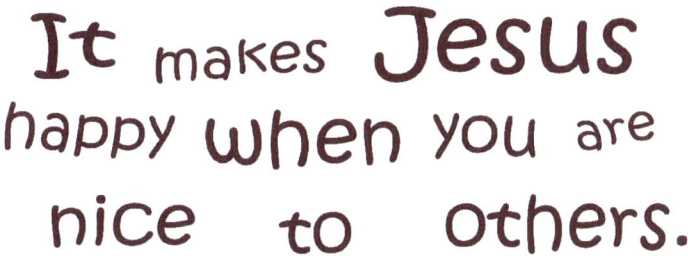

It makes Jesus happy when you are nice to others.

(Taken from Ephesians 4:32)

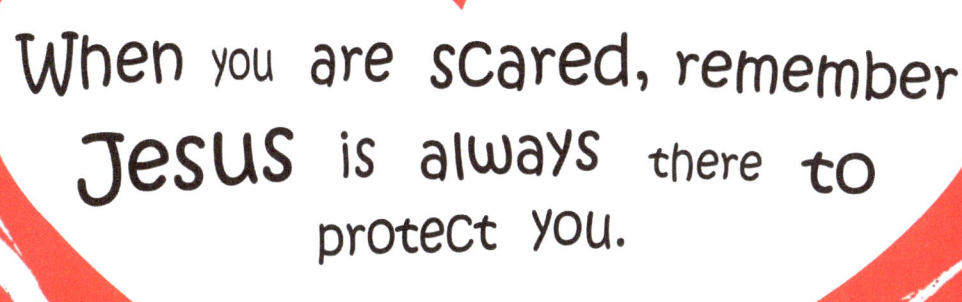

When you are scared, remember Jesus is always there to protect you.

(Taken from Isaiah 40:10)

When things seem bad, Jesus will always be there for you and never leave you.

(Taken from Psalm 50:15)

Jesus loves everyone.

(Taken from John 3:16)

When someone makes you mad or sad,

Jesus wants you to forgive them.
(Taken from Ephesians 4:32)

23 Even if another child thinks you look funny,

remember Jesus still thinks you are perfect.
(Taken from Genesis 1:27)

When your parents ask you to brush your teeth, it makes Jesus happy when you listen and obey them.

(Taken from Colossians 3:20)

Jesus wants you to always remember He loves you so much, will never leave you and is always there for you.

29 The end. Thank you and God bless.

Dedication and Appreciations

Laura, my loving and supportive wife.

Charlie and Jack, my sons who my wife and I will lead to the Lord.

Jim and Tanna, my parents who led me to the Lord by example.

Bill Wilson, established author who provided me with guidance.

For more information please visit
www.myjesusbook.com

www.ingramcontent.com/pod-product-compliance
Lightning Source LLC
Chambersburg PA
CBHW041154290426
44108CB00002B/65